T0017016

All About Insects

An illustrated guide to bugs and creepy-crawlies

ARCTURUS

ARCTURUS

This edition published in 2022 by Arcturus Publishing Limited
26/27 Bickels Yard, 151–153 Bermondsey Street,
London SE1 3HA

Copyright © Arcturus Holdings Limited
All rights reserved. No part of this publication may be reproduced, stored in a
retrieval system, or transmitted, in any form or by any means, electronic, mechanical,
photocopying, recording, or otherwise, without prior written permission in
accordance with the provisions of the Copyright Act 1956 (as amended). Any
person or persons who do any unauthorized act in relation to this publication may
be liable to criminal prosecution and civil claims for damages.
Author: Polly Cheeseman
Illustrator: Iris Deppe
Designer: Stefan Holliland
Editor: Violet Peto
Consultant: Anne Rooney
Managing Editor: Joe Harris

ISBN: 978-1-3988-1993-1
CH010042NT
Supplier 29, Date 0622, PI 00002185

Printed in China

Contents

Creepy-Crawlies 4

Incredible Insects 6

Beautiful Beetles 8

Watery World 10

Butterfly Life Cycle 12

Make a Butterfly Feeder 14

Praying Mantis 16

Under Attack 18

Making Honey 20

Hairy Hunters 22

Glow in the Dark 24

Bugs in Hiding 26

Teamwork 28

Dung Beetles 30

On the Forest Floor 32

Amazing Journey 34

Building Bugs 36

Slithering Along 38

Make a Bug Hotel 40

Cunning Predators 42

Swarm of Locusts 44

Why We Need Bugs 46

Glossary 48

Creepy-Crawlies

Most animals on Earth are **invertebrates**, that is, animals without a backbone or skeleton inside their bodies. Take a look around you—there are all kinds of invertebrates everywhere!

Wasp

Arthropods are invertebrates that have a tough outer layer to their bodies instead of a skeleton. This is called an **exoskeleton**. There are different types of arthropods.

Crustaceans are arthropods with 10 or more legs. Many crustaceans, such as lobsters and crabs, live in water. But wood lice are crustaceans, too!

Beetle

Wood lice

Most of the creatures that people call creepy-crawlies, such as bees, beetles, and butterflies, are **insects**. They usually have wings, six jointed legs, and three parts to their bodies.

Arachnids are also arthropods. Most arachnids have eight jointed legs and two body sections. Spiders, scorpions, and mites are all arachnids.

Garden spider

There are a huge number of other kinds of invertebrates. Many soft-bodied invertebrates live underwater, but snails, slugs, and worms slither around on land.

Incredible Insects

How would you like to walk upside down on the ceiling, or have eyes as big as your head? **Insects** come in many shapes and sizes, and even the common housefly has amazing abilities.

Insects have **compound eyes**, which are made up of thousands of tiny parts. Compound eyes let insects spot quick movements around them.

A housefly's huge compound eyes cover most of its head. They give the fly a very wide view. It can even see behind itself!

Compound eye

Head

Thorax

Antenna

Abdomen

An insect's body has three parts—the head, **thorax**, and **abdomen**. The two feelers on its head, called **antennae**, are used to smell, touch, or taste.

Most insects have wings. Flies can beat their wings hundreds of times a second. They can fly forward, backward, hover, and flip over to land upside down!

Beautiful Beetles

With around 40,000 different types, beetles form the largest group of **insects**. Beetles live all over the world, in scorching hot and freezing cold places. They can also be found in the park or your own backyard!

Flying wings

Most beetles have two pairs of wings and can fly. The front wing cases are tough and fold over the delicate back wings.

In order to fly, the beetle's wing cases move apart and its long flying wings unfold. Beetles can look a little clumsy when they fly!

Although they look pretty, some kinds of leaf beetles can damage plants. The striped cucumber beetle is seen as a pest because it destroys farmers' crops.

Wing case

Known as ladybirds, ladybugs, or lady beetles, these red, spotted beetles often visit backyards. Gardeners love them, because they eat aphids that destroy plants.

Some beetles' wing cases are bright and patterned. This acts as a warning to other creatures that the beetle is **poisonous**, or tastes bad.

Aphids

Weevils are a type of beetle with a long snout. The beautiful Schoenherr's blue weevil lives on the island of New Guinea, in the Pacific Ocean.

Watery World

Many different creatures visit ponds and lakes to find food and lay their eggs. Some **insects** spend the first part of their lives in water, before coming to the surface to breathe air as adults.

Dragonflies dart over the water's surface.

Backswimmers swim on their backs, using their long legs to "row" themselves near the surface. They hold a bubble of air under their wings, so they can breathe underwater.

Rams-horn snails live in fresh water, but they need to come to the surface to breathe air. They breathe through their skin.

Red-winged blackbird

Roseate skimmer dragonfly

Whirligig beetles
swim in circles on the surface.
These beetles have two pairs
of eyes—one pair looks
up, and the other pair
looks down underwater.

Young dragonflies, called **nymphs**,
live underwater. When they're fully
grown, they climb out and change
into adult dragonflies.

Dragonfly
nymph

11

Butterfly Life Cycle

Butterflies go through four different stages in their lives. At the end of each stage, they completely change the way they look and act.
The full sequence of an animal's life is called a **life cycle**.

1

Butterflies lay their eggs on leaves.

Egg

4

Inside the cocoon, the caterpillar changes into a butterfly!

This incredible change is called **metamorphosis**.

Spicebush swallowtail

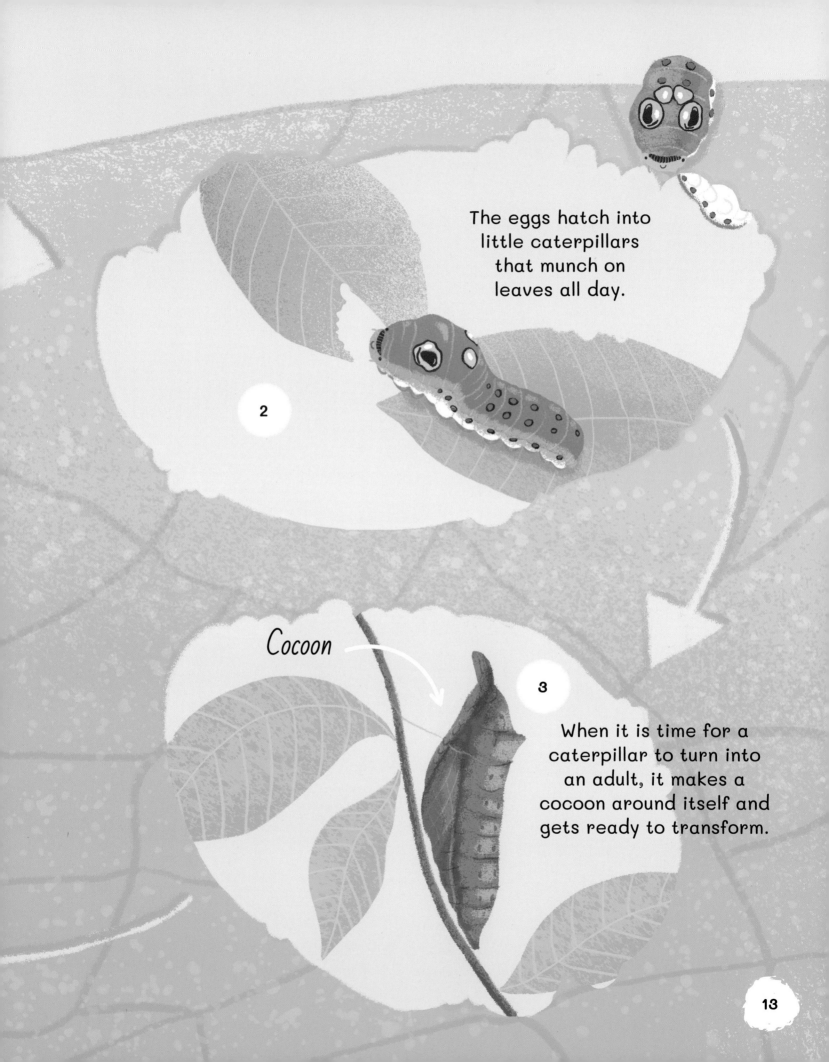

The eggs hatch into little caterpillars that munch on leaves all day.

2

Cocoon

3

When it is time for a caterpillar to turn into an adult, it makes a cocoon around itself and gets ready to transform.

Make a Butterfly Feeder

Butterflies feed on liquids. They suck up **nectar** from flowers using a curled mouthpart called a **proboscis**. Bring butterflies fluttering to your backyard with this sweet feeder.

1

Use the lid of a large food container or a paper plate for your feeder. Decorate it with a few bright flower shapes using felt-tip pens or paint.

2

Ask an adult to make four equally-spaced holes close to the rim of your feeder. A hole punch is ideal for this.

3

Thread string through the hole and knot to secure. Repeat with the other holes. Gather the four loose ends of string and knot together.

Put chopped fruit onto each flower on your feeder. Use whatever soft fruit you have—the riper, the better.

4

Hang your feeder outside by its string ... and wait!

Red admiral

Holly blue

Tortoiseshell

Do the butterflies prefer a particular fruit?

Try making some sweet liquid by mixing sugar with water. Fill the lid of a jar or bottle with the sugar-water and place on your feeder.

Praying Mantis

It may look like a leaf, but this **insect** is actually a fearsome **predator**. The mantis has two long front legs, which it holds in front of itself as if in prayer.

The praying mantis can turn its head all the way around to look behind it and all around. Its huge eyes spot the slightest movement.

The mantis keeps very still. When an insect comes close, it strikes suddenly with lightning speed. The two front legs shoot out and grab the **prey**.

Many are green to help them hide in leafy surroundings. Some mantises are brown, so that they look like dead leaves, or pink so they look like flowers.

Common praying mantis

The front legs have spines and hooks to grip struggling prey. The mantis starts eating its victim immediately.

17

Under Attack

Insects and other creepy-crawlies make a tasty meal for lots of different animals. Some bugs warn **predators** with the way they look. Others have clever ways to defend themselves.

Ant

Bombardier beetles can be found all over the world. These small beetles live on the ground, among fallen leaves and under stones.

When attacked, a bombardier beetle mixes two chemicals together inside its body. Then, a boiling liquid shoots out of its **abdomen** with a loud "pop."

The bombardier beetle's liquid weapon is **poisonous**, as well as scalding hot. It is powerful enough to blind or kill a would-be attacker. Luckily, it does not kill humans.

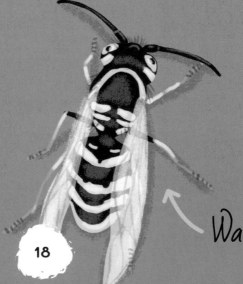

Bees and wasps can give a nasty sting to any creature that bothers them. At first glance, a hoverfly looks like a bee or wasp, so animals keep away.

Wasp

Hoverfly

Bombardier beetle

The bombardier beetle can even direct its spray and aim at a predator. The beetle can fire 20 times before it runs out of liquid.

Stink bugs get their name from the strong smell they make if they are attacked. The man-faced stink bug has markings that warn predators they taste bad, too.

Fuzzy caterpillars can look pretty or cute, but beware. The saddleback caterpillar has stinging spines on its body that inject a painful venom.

19

Making Honey

While some types of bees live on their own, honeybees live in groups called colonies. There can be many thousands of bees in a colony, and each has its own role to play.

The "queen" is the mother of all the bees in the nest and is the largest. Her job is laying eggs.

The nest is made up of honeycomb. The honeycomb contains hexagonal "cells."

Larva

Most bees are female "workers." Their job is looking after the hive, the **larvae** (baby bees), and the queen. There are a few males called drones.

Egg

Nest

Workers suck up **nectar** from flowers, which turns into honey inside them. They spit the honey into the cells. The honey feeds the colony.

A larva is the wormlike form that hatches from an egg. The workers feed it, and when it is big enough, they seal it inside the cell. The larva slowly changes into a bee. It is called a **pupa** at this stage. Finally, it breaks out of its cell as an adult bee.

Hairy Hunters

Spiders can be teeny-tiny or huge and hairy!
The largest spiders in the world are tarantulas.
Most tarantulas live in warm forests, where they
hunt **insects**, frogs, and other small creatures.

A tarantula's body is covered
with hairs that sense movements
in the air. Tiny hairs and claws
on the bottom of its feet help the
tarantula run and climb.

With eight long legs,
spiders can run very
fast. Tarantulas often
hide in their underground
burrows. When **prey**
comes near, they leap
out to attack.

Tarantulas use their two fangs to
inject prey with venom. The venom
keeps the prey from moving and
turns its insides into liquid, which
the spider sucks up.

Mexican red-kneed tarantula

Unlike many other spiders, tarantulas do not spin webs. Many tarantulas use their silk to line their burrows. They pull the silk from their bodies using their back legs.

23

Glow in the Dark

Many creepy-crawlies come out at night to avoid being seen, but fireflies do the opposite! These glowing **insects** put on an amazing light show that can be seen for miles.

Also known as lightning bugs, fireflies are not flies or bugs, but beetles. There are more than a thousand different types of fireflies.

To make light, the firefly mixes chemicals in a special organ in its **abdomen**. An animal that can make its own light is said to be bioluminescent.

Fireflies glow to attract a **mate**. Different types of fireflies make their own special light shows. Some flash on and off in a pattern, while others keep glowing.

A firefly's light may also act as a warning signal to **predators**. If eaten, a firefly has a bitter taste and can make some animals sick.

Male European glowworms look like ordinary beetles. At night, the flightless females climb up plant stems and start to glow, in order to attract a mate.

Bugs in Hiding

Some creatures can blend in with their surroundings to help them hide from **predators**—or **prey**. A relative of the walking stick, or stick insect, the leaf insect is one of the best camouflaged animals of all!

It's really hard to spot a leaf insect because it looks almost exactly like a leaf! It can hide in plain sight of predators, such as birds and reptiles.

When resting, the blue morpho butterfly closes its bright, blue wings. The undersides of its wings are brown and patterned, so they blend in with the forest floor.

The crab spider perfectly matches the flower it hides in. It waits for **insects** to visit the flower, then attacks.

Leaf insects live in forests, eating the leaves of the plants they live on. Sometimes, leaf insects accidentally take a bite out of each other!

Some leaf insects have brown markings that make them even more realistic. Others are completely brown and look like dead leaves.

Leaf

Leaf insect

Leaf insects usually stay still to avoid being spotted. When they do walk, they sway their bodies and look like real leaves blowing in the breeze.

Sometimes called a jumping stick, the stick grasshopper has a long, twiglike body and legs. It is perfectly camouflaged—until it jumps!

Teamwork

Like honeybees, ants live in **colonies**, and each member does a certain job. An ant colony can contain millions of ants. All the ants work together to keep the colony going.

Worker ant

Soldier ant

Larva

Most ants live in nests made from soil, leaves, wood, or sand. Army ants are different—most of the time they are on the move.

Army ants are blind, so they use their long **antennae** to find their way. The ants feed on any creature they come across, attacking with their powerful jaws.

As they travel, workers carry the eggs and **larvae**. Larger "soldier" ants protect them. If there's a gap to pass, army ants form a "bridge" with their bodies.

The queen lays all the eggs in the colony. Workers feed and protect the queen and her larvae. With no fixed nest, the ants make their own temporary shelter. Many ants hold onto each other, making a ball protecting those inside!

Dung Beetles

Dung beetles depend on the droppings of larger animals. They roll animal poop, live in it, lay their eggs in it, and eat it! There are thousands of different kinds of dung beetles living all over the world.

Dung beetles have an excellent sense of smell, sniffing out animal poop from great distances! The dung contains all the water and **nutrients** the beetle needs.

When a beetle finds dung, it rolls it into a ball larger than itself. Then, it rolls the dung ball away using its strong back legs.

For its size, a dung beetle is one of the strongest creatures on Earth. It can move a dung ball that is hundreds of times its own body weight!

Some beetles burrow into the dung ball, eating it from the inside. Females lay their eggs in the middle. When they hatch, the **larvae** eat the dung around them.

By recycling animal poop, dung beetles do an important job. They are natural cleaners, keeping animal dung from piling up and keeping flies at bay!

Dung beetles belong to the family of beetles called scarabs, which were held in high praise by the ancient Egyptians. There are many thousands of types of scarab beetles, and some are very beautiful.

On the Forest Floor

Next time you go for a walk in the woods, don't forget to look down. There are many small creatures that make their homes among the fallen leaves and dead wood.

Stag beetles scuttle over logs and stumps, feeding on tree sap. Male stag beetles use their antler-like jaws to attract females and fight enemies.

European stag beetle

Chicken of the woods fungus

Lift up a log, and you'll probably find wood lice underneath. These little **crustaceans** eat rotting wood and plants. They like damp, dark places.

Silver-washed fritillary

Earwigs are found in leaf litter and under bark. They have long pincers on the end of their **abdomens**, which they use to defend themselves.

Moss

Centipedes are **arthropods**. They spend the day hiding in soil or under dead wood. At night, they use their **venomous** fangs to catch insects, worms, and spiders.

Amazing Journey

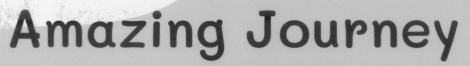

Every year, millions of monarch butterflies fly up to 4,800 km (3,000 miles) from Canada to Mexico. This incredible journey is called a **migration**. No other butterfly travels as far.

The journey south takes around two months. Monarchs save energy by gliding on air currents. They stop on the way, to rest and drink **nectar**.

Monarchs must avoid being eaten by **predators**, such as birds. If the weather is too wet, cold, or windy, they cannot fly. Some do not survive.

When they finally arrive in Mexico, the butterflies rest on fir trees for the winter. Millions of monarch butterflies cover the trees in a blanket of orange.

Monarch butterflies only live for a few months. Those that migrate have never made the journey before. No one knows for sure how they find their way.

In the spring, monarch butterflies fly the long journey north again. Once they have laid their eggs, the butterflies die.

Building Bugs

Some creepy-crawlies are capable of making incredible structures! Termites are tiny **insects** that live in large **colonies**. Together, they create towering nests that change the landscape.

Chimney

Eggs and young

Queen

Termite colonies are made up of one queen and many workers. As well as looking after the queen, eggs, and babies, the workers build the nest.

Workers mix soil with spit and poop to build mounds. Gradually, the mounds get bigger, harder, and taller. Some termite mounds are 5 m (17 ft) tall!

The Darwin's bark spider from Madagascar spins the largest web of any spider. Its web can stretch across a river, trapping insects in superstrong silk.

Weaver ants build their nests in trees. The ants push leaves together, weaving the edges with silk made by their **larvae**.

Inside the mound is a network of corridors and chambers for the queen and the young. A chimney runs through the middle, bringing fresh air inside.

Queen

Workers

The huge queen termite never leaves the mound. She can grow to be the length of a human finger—100 times bigger than a worker!

The caddisfly larva lives underwater. For protection, it builds a case around itself. It spins together sand, shells, twigs, and leaves with a silk it makes.

Slithering Along

If you go for a walk after a rain shower, you may see slugs, snails, and worms slithering about. These soft-bodied invertebrates must keep their skin damp in order to survive.

A snail has a shell on its back and hides inside when in danger. The shell grows with the snail, so it always fits perfectly.

Eye stalks

Slugs and snails move along on a muscular "foot." Their eyes are on the end of long stalks. Two feelers taste the air and ground in front.

Slugs and snails have tongues covered with thousands of tiny teeth. They eat plants, scraping and filing them with their toothy tongues.

Slime is very important for slugs and snails. It helps them slide along, stick to surfaces, and keeps their bodies from drying out.

Slime trail

Feelers

Earthworms eat rotting leaves and dead plants, recycling them into soil. They also mix air and water into soil, helping plants grow.

Make a Bug Hotel

Get up close to creepy-crawlies, and make a mini bug hotel for your backyard. You'll need a clean, empty drink carton, some kitchen or toilet paper tubes, and lots of natural materials.

1

Ask an adult to help you cut out a rectangle from one side of your carton, leaving 2 cm (1 in) around the edges.

2

Cut some pieces of cardboard tubes, so that they fit into the carton with the holes facing outward. Fill the carton with the tubes.

3

When the carton is tightly packed with tubes, add your natural materials. Try using twigs, bark, dry leaves, moss, grass, and stones.

4

Find a sheltered place for your bug hotel—perhaps by a fence or under a bush. Check every day to see if any bug buddies have checked in!

Why not paint or decorate your bug hotel?

Cunning Predators

Not all bugs are happy to chomp through plants and leaves—some prefer a meatier meal. Assassin bugs are creepy-crawly killers with very unusual hunting habits.

Assassin bugs are the fierce **predators** of the **insect** world, which is how they get their name. They often hunt by sneaking up on their **prey**.

The trapdoor spider's burrow has a hinged lid made from silk and soil. When it senses prey, the spider bursts through the trapdoor and attacks.

The assassin bug stabs and injects saliva (spit) into prey using its sharp mouthparts. The prey's insides turn to liquid, which the assassin sucks up.

After it has eaten, a young ant-eating assassin bug piles empty ant bodies on its back. It can carry 20 ants at a time!

The ants are held with sticky threads that the bug makes on its back. It's believed that this strange disguise puts off would-be attackers.

The Amazonian giant centipede hunts in caves by hanging from the ceiling. It will catch a bat as it flies, killing it with its **venomous** fangs.

Swarm of Locusts

When animals gather together in huge numbers, it is called a swarm. A locust is the name for a type of grasshopper that swarms with devastating effects.

Locusts are **insects** with strong back legs, making them great at jumping. They rub their legs on their wings to create a loud chirping noise.

Locusts spend most of the time alone. However, changes in the weather and a lack of food can make locusts look and behave differently.

The locusts gather together, forming a large swarm of millions of insects. The swarm flies huge distances for days or weeks at a time.

When the swarm lands, the locusts eat any plants they find. The hungry insects can completely strip and destroy farmers' crops.

Midges are tiny flies that swarm in order to find a **mate**. They form shimmering, cloud-like swarms in the early evening, often near water.

Why We Need Bugs

Although some can bite or sting, and others can eat our plants, **insects** and creepy-crawlies are an important part of nature. We cannot live without them!

Many animals, such as birds, small mammals, and reptiles, depend on insects and other bugs for their food.

Insects are a great source of food for people, too. In some cultures, bugs are considered a delicious snack. We also farm bees for the sweet honey they make.

Some insects, such as butterflies, bees, and moths are pollinators. This means that they help plants grow new ones by spreading their **pollen** from flower to flower.

Insects can help us by eating bugs that harm our crops and gardens.

Invertebrates such as worms and beetles help break down dead plants, recycling **nutrients** back into the soil.

47

GLOSSARY

Abdomen The rear part of an insect's or spider's body.

Antennae An invertebrate's feelers, used for sensing.

Arachnid An arthropod with eight legs, such as a spider, scorpion, or mite.

Arthropod An invertebrate with jointed legs, exoskeleton, and a body divided into segments.

Colony A group of animals that live together.

Compound eye An eye that is made up of many tiny lenses, rather than just one.

Crustacean A type of arthropod such as a crab or lobster. Most crustaceans live in the sea, but wood lice live on land.

Exoskeleton A hard outer skeleton.

Insect An arthropod with six legs and three body parts.

Invertebrate An animal that has no bony skeleton inside its body.

Larvae Insects or other creatures in their very young form.

Life cycle The growth and life of a living thing from birth to death

Mate An animal's partner for breeding.

Metamorphosis The change from one form into another.

Migration A seasonal journey that an animal makes in order to feed, breed, or escape the cold.

Nectar A sweet liquid produced by flowers that animals like to eat.

Nymph The early stage of some animals' lives before they grow into their adult form.

Nutrients Substances that are important for the growth and development of plants and animals.

Poisonous Contains substances that are harmful when touched or eaten.

Pollen A sticky powder that plants produce to make more plants.

Predator An animal that hunts and eats other animals.

Prey An animal that is hunted and eaten by other animals.

Proboscis A tube-like mouthpart used by some insects to suck up liquids.

Pupa A stage in the life cycle of some insects when they change from a larva into an adult.

Thorax The middle part of an insect's body.

Venomous Contains substances that are harmful when injected into another animal by biting or stinging.